KENNETH COPELAND

MW01093200

Receive as a
CHILD

Live Like a
KING

KENNETH
COPELAND
PUBLICATIONS

Unless otherwise noted, all scripture is from the *King James Version* of the Bible.

Scripture quotations marked *The Amplified Bible* are from *The Amplified Bible, Old Testament* © 1965, 1987 by the Zondervan Corporation. *The Amplified New Testament* © 1958, 1987 by The Lockman Foundation. Used by permission.

Receive as a Child, Live Like a King
Knowing and Receiving Your Inheritance

ISBN 978-1-60463-109-8   30-0070

18 17 16 15 14 13   9 8 7 6 5 4

© 1999 Eagle Mountain International Church Inc. aka Kenneth Copeland Ministries

Kenneth Copeland Publications
Fort Worth, TX 76192-0001

For more information about Kenneth Copeland Ministries, visit kcm.org or call 1-800-600-7395 (U.S. only) or +1-817-852-6000.

Receive as a Child,
Live Like a King

From the time I was 6 years old, I wanted a motorcycle. I dreamed about motorcycles all the time.

I can remember coming home from school when I was a boy, and as I would turn the last corner before I could see our house, I would cover my eyes so I couldn't see the yard. Then I'd tell myself, *There's going to be a motorcycle in that yard.*

Day after day, I hid my eyes. Day after day, I pretended I would see a motorcycle sitting there. Day after day, I never did. So I just kept dreaming.

Like most kids I knew, I grew up thinking that, if there was something I wanted and I had to ask my parents for it, then I could count on having a hard time getting it...like a motorcycle, for instance. Why was that?

Well, if you think about it, probably generations of children have been raised on, "No, not now!" and, "What do you need that for, anyway?"

Today, you can go into any department

store, toy store or grocery store and hear some parent say, "No, no...put that back—we can't afford that!" or, "What do you think I'm made of—money?"

I don't care whether they're rich or poor, Christian or non-Christian, that's the general attitude a lot of parents communicate when their children come to them asking for something. What's more, most of those parents probably don't mean to be that way.

It's no surprise, then, to realize that generations of Christians have been raised in church believing it's next to impossible to get anything from God.

Now, I was raised in a wonderful, godly home by parents who were givers. They tithed on everything that came into their hands from the day they were married. They never did without, either. Yet, from the way I was raised at home and what I was taught in church, I assumed it was next to impossible to get anything from God.

You see, for centuries, the Church focused on scriptures such as Romans 3:23—"For all have sinned, and come short of the glory of God." Preachers majored on our falling short of God's glory. In sermon after sermon, we heard how we needed to become God's servants and humble ourselves as slaves before Him.

Do you realize our servitude doesn't mean a thing to God? It really doesn't. Not until we take our place as His children, first.

When you and I were born again, we didn't become God's servants. We became His children, which was what He was after all along. We became children of the King, sons and daughters of the Most High God. And because of that, we gained access to a glorious inheritance—one that we didn't have to wait until heaven to receive.

Today, however, the Church is not walking in and enjoying the fullness of its rightful inheritance—all the blessings promised to us through our spiritual father, Abraham. The reason we're not is because we've not known our true identity. We haven't received our sonship in the kingdom of God.

Servant or Son?

When it comes to inheritance and serving God, we've all probably heard plenty of preaching on the parable of the prodigal son, and most of it probably focused on the son who squandered his father's money. But there's another point to that story about a father and his two sons. It's not just about the son who got into trouble.

The parable begins in Luke 15:11-16:

> A certain man had two sons: And the younger of them said to his father, Father, give me the portion of goods that falleth to me. And he divided unto them his living. And not many days after the younger son gathered all together, and took his journey into a far country, and there wasted his substance with riotous living. And when he had spent all, there arose a mighty famine in that land; and he began to be in want. And he went and joined himself to a citizen of that country; and he sent him into his fields to feed swine. And he would fain have filled his belly with the husks that the swine did eat: and no man gave unto him.

It was the younger son who went to his father and asked for his inher-itance. But notice how this bold request didn't seem to upset the father in the least. That's an important detail we need to keep in mind as we study this passage.

After the father divided his holdings and gave his younger son what was rightfully his, the first thing this young fellow did with his newfound wealth was hit the road. He went looking for a good time. The only problem was, he didn't have the wisdom to handle all his riches. Consequently, his riotous living came to a sobering end—in a pigpen.

When it finally dawned on the young man that the hogs he tended were eating better than he was, he came to his senses. Then he came up with a plan, which we find in verses 18-19: "I will arise and go to my father, and will say unto him, Father, I have sinned against heaven, and before thee, and am no more worthy to be called thy son: make me as one of thy hired servants."

The way this son figured it, his father's servants were better off than he was. So, if he could just go back home, humble himself before his father and get hired on as one of "the help," he'd be doing pretty good.

It was a good plan. What's more, it

worked...that is, up to a point.

When the prodigal son went home, his father met him before he even made it back to the house. The repentant son confessed his error and told his father how wrong he had been and how unworthy he was to be called a son. But then the plan began to fall apart.

Before the son could throw himself at his father's mercy, and ask to be made a servant, the father interrupted: "Bring forth the best robe, and put it on him; and put a ring on his hand, and shoes on his feet: And bring hither the fatted calf, and kill it; and let us eat, and be merry: For this my son was dead, and is alive again; he was lost, and is found" (verses 22-24).

Now, let me ask you this: Had the prodigal son been able to carry out his plan, do you think his father would have agreed to it?

No, certainly not! Just look at his response.

This father was thrilled to have his boy back, pig smell and all. In fact, he was probably so busy kissing and hugging and just looking at his boy that he never even heard a word his son said.

Reduce his long-lost son to the status of servant?

Nonsense!

But notice this. Here's the son, working up enough nerve to ask his father if he can come back home and live as one of the servants, and the whole time he's trying to ease into the question, his father is busy barking orders to all the servants—"Get this...get that! Do this...do that!" The man has servants hopping all over the place.

This man already had servants. The prodigal son even said so himself: "How many hired servants of my father's have bread enough and to spare" (verse 17).

If the man had many servants, what did he need with another one?

No, on this particular day, when the father looked "a great way off," he wasn't looking for another servant. He had servants. What he lacked was s-o-n-s. He was looking for a son...and a son was what he got.

Servitude or Sonship?

The prodigal son never got his opportunity to become a servant, at least not the way he had planned. His plan actually backfired on him, but in a good way. Before he knew what had happened, he was wearing a robe and a ring and was sitting down to a feast in his honor. That meant he was back in the family. He was a son once again.

In teaching His followers, Jesus could have ended the parable on this happy note, but He didn't. It was only half the story.

The rest of the story is in Luke 15:25-30. It's the part about the other son.

> Now his elder son was in the field: and as he came and drew nigh to the house, he heard music and dancing. And he called one of the servants, and asked what these things meant. And he said unto him, Thy brother is come; and thy father hath killed the fatted calf, because he hath received him safe and sound. And he was angry, and would not go in: therefore came his father out, and entreated him. And he answering said to his father, Lo, these many years do I serve thee, neither transgressed I at any time thy commandment: and yet thou never gavest me a kid, that I might make merry with my friends: But as soon as this thy son was come,

which hath devoured thy living with harlots, thou hast killed for him the fatted calf.

First, notice that while all the celebrating was going on, the elder son was out in the fields. He wasn't up at the big house running the family business as he should have been, especially since everything left was his. No, he was out in the fields working in the dirt.

This is an important detail because Jesus is trying to get something over to us about the attitude of these two sons.

When the elder son finally arrived on the scene, to the sounds of merrymaking, and found out what had happened...he was upset. That's when his true heart—and mindset— were revealed.

"Lo, these many years do I serve thee," he told his father (verse 29).

Here's the elder son trying to be a servant, too. But he's not just trying to be a servant— he's already thinking like one, talking like one and acting like one. All the while, everything his father owns—including all the servants— belongs to him.

So this father, who probably had more

servants than he could keep track of, had sons. Yet, his sons were trying to be servants. Both were sons. Both had position and inheritance. But neither took his rightful place as a son. Neither of them truly stepped into his inheritance as a son.

Certainly, the father had given them their inheritance, but neither one received it in honor. The younger son took his and spent it in dishonor. The elder son never recognized the fact that all his father had was his (Luke 15:31). He was out in the field trying to make everybody happy by working hard.

So, truthfully, the father in this parable had no sons. He did—yet—he didn't. He really only had servants.

It's All in the Will

Like the father in Jesus' parable, God is wanting sons. Hebrews 2:10 tells us that "it became [God]...in bringing many sons unto glory." Indeed, if we're born again, you and I truly are the sons and daughters of Almighty God.

For the most part, the problem in the Church has been that we've been too busy trying to serve God. We've been thinking and speaking and acting like servants, not sons.

"Well, Brother Copeland, are you saying we're not supposed to serve God?"

No, I'm simply drawing attention to what Jesus revealed as wrong thinking on the part of the prodigal son and his brother.

It's one thing to know you're a son of the Most High God—as Jesus Himself was well aware—and then to go humbly before your heavenly Father and say, "Father, I know I'm Your son. I know what all I have inherited by Jesus' blood and Name and by The Word. But I want You to know I'll do anything You need or want me to do. I'll do anything to bring glory to You."

That's essentially what Jesus did before the foundation of the world when He offered Himself to the Father as the sacrifice necessary to redeem mankind.

It is another matter, however, to cry out to God and say, "Oh, Lord, I'm such a worm. I'm so unworthy of Your love and grace. But, Lord, You know how hard I've worked as Your humble servant down here...."

Just think—here's God, wanting to bring "many sons unto glory," but we're all too busy working hard out in the fields. Meanwhile, God has more angels serving Him than we could probably count in a lifetime. He even has angels that do nothing but fly around Him day and night declaring, "Holy, holy, holy!"

So what does He need with more servants?

We read in Galatians 4:4-7, "God sent forth his Son, made of a woman, made under the law, to redeem them that were under the law, that we might receive the adoption of sons. And because ye are sons, God hath sent forth the Spirit of his Son into your hearts, crying, Abba, Father. Wherefore thou art no more a servant, but a son; and if a son, then an heir of God through Christ."

The Apostle Paul was especially aware of this revelation of our sonship in the kingdom of God. As we find in Acts 26, during his encounter with Jesus on the road to Damascus, the Lord specifically told him:

I have appeared unto thee for this purpose, to make thee a minister and a witness both of these things which thou hast seen, and of those things in the which I will appear unto thee;

delivering thee from the people, and from the Gentiles, unto whom now I send thee, to open their eyes, and to turn them from darkness to light, and from the power of Satan unto God, that they may receive forgiveness of sins, and inheritance..." (verses 16-18).

In other words, Jesus was telling Paul, "They've inherited something, and I want them to know it. I want them to know their sins have been forgiven. I want them to know the devil doesn't have power over them anymore. I want them to know that they have an inheritance in My Name and by My blood— and I want you to tell them!"

Dusting Off Unclaimed Wealth

What good is such a glorious inheritance if you and I never receive it?

Paul told believers at Ephesus the same thing he wrote to the Galatians. But he added, "Having predestinated us unto the adoption of children by Jesus Christ to himself.... in whom also we have obtained an inheritance" (Ephesians 1:5, 11).

We don't have to wait until we die and go to heaven to receive our inheritance. We obtained our inherit-ance when Jesus died. It's available to us right now!

In fact, Jesus is the only man ever to write a will, die, then come back from the grave and probate, or officially validate, His own will.

Even at this very moment, Jesus is watching over that will—the new covenant bought by His blood—seeing to it that every letter and every detail of it is kept for our benefit.

All that sounds wonderful, yet generations of Christians have never laid claim to what rightfully belonged to them.

I heard about a young woman in Tulsa, Oklahoma, who had come into a sizable inheritance, but she never knew it. One day, a friend saw her name listed in a newspaper ad along with several others. A bank was trying to locate these people to let them know they had money in old accounts that had been left unclaimed.

When the young woman first learned of the advertisement, she thought her friend was teasing. But sure enough, her name was in the paper. When she contacted the bank, they informed her that she had received an inheritance from a family member and it had been deposited into an account. No one in the woman's family had ever told her about the inheritance, so the money just sat there in the bank.

Today, many born-again, Holy Spirit-baptized, Bible-wagging believers have no idea of the full extent of their redemption. They have no concept of all that is available to them—now!

Romans 8:16-17 says, "The Spirit itself beareth witness with our spirit, that we are the children of God: and if children, then heirs; heirs of God, and joint-heirs with Christ."

Notice the Apostle Paul did not say we are co-heirs with the Anointed One. Rather, he said we are joint heirs, and that's important.

Let's say a man had 100 acres of land and two children. If he were to leave 50 acres to each child in his will, then they would be co-heirs. Each child would only receive half of the estate.

Joint heir, on the other hand, is like the joint tax return or joint bank account of a husband and wife. Each has access to the entire tax return or bank account. Each owns all of the money, not just half of it.

Paul goes on to explain in Philippians 4:15-17 that we have a heavenly account.

> Now ye Philippians know also, that in the beginning of the gospel, when I departed from Macedonia, no church communicated with me as concerning giving and receiving, but ye only. For even in Thessalonica ye sent once and again unto my necessity. Not because I desire a gift: but I desire fruit that may abound to your account.

When we tithe and honor God with the firstfruit of our income, God in turn opens an account and honors us with His fruit. Throughout the Bible, we read that God is the multiplier of the fruit.

"Well, you know, Brother Copeland, we must be good stewards of God's money."

It's not God's money we're dealing with here. This is our money.

In the parable of the prodigal son, the father told the elder son, "All that I have is thine" (Luke 15:31). The elder son was jealous of the younger one, who had squandered all his inheritance on riotous living, yet all the while he never realized all that remained was his. He was treating it as though it were his father's, and not his own.

So, Paul was talking about our account, our money—fruit that may abound to our account.

Consequently, you and I have every right to our heavenly accounts—to our inheritance as sons and daughters of God. But we need to understand how to make withdrawals from those accounts. After all, our names may be in the newspaper, but if we don't know how to go to the bank and make a withdrawal, our inheritance will just sit there...unclaimed.

Taking Into Account Heaven's Riches

To help us lay hold of our inherit-ance, and all that rightfully belongs to us, I want us to study seven steps taken straight from The Word of God. These steps will enable us to tap into and begin enjoying our full inheritance as joint heirs with Jesus.

The first three steps are found in 1 Timothy 6:17-19.

Charge them that are rich in this world, that they be not highminded, nor trust in uncertain riches, but in the living God, who giveth us richly all things to enjoy; that they do good, that they be rich in good works, ready to distribute, willing to communicate; laying up in store for themselves a good foundation against the time to come, that they may lay hold on eternal life.

Step 1—Don't trust in uncertain riches.

Verse 17 says, "Charge them that are rich in this world, that they be not highminded, nor trust in uncertain riches, but in the living God, who giveth us richly all things to enjoy."

God gave us an account so we could enjoy all the things He's given us. He didn't give us wealth to grieve over, which is what the rich young ruler did in Matthew 19. He was very rich, yet grew sorrowful at the idea of giving. As a result, his grief separated him from God. He turned his back on Jesus' offer to follow

Him, all because he had possessions. He trusted in his riches.

We need to stop being possessive of our possessions and stop trying to run our own finances. That's what gets us into messes, especially when we think we have a lot. Because, once we start thinking we have great possessions, we can easily become "highminded."

In *The Amplified Bible, highminded* is translated as "proud and arrogant and contemptuous of others." We have nothing to be arrogant about when we consider the fact that God uses gold for street pavement in heaven. Our handful of earthly possessions doesn't compare.

Step 2—Be willing to communicate.

Going back to 1 Timothy 6, we read in verse 18, "...That they do good, that they be rich in good works, ready to distribute, willing to communicate."

Here the word *communicate* simply means to give and receive.

When you have a conversation with someone, you both must be able to speak (give) and to listen (receive). In this verse, though the principle of communication is the same, what's being communicated is different. Instead of words or thoughts or ideas flowing back and forth between people, it's good works—riches, possessions, goods, money, etc.—that are being transmitted and received.

When it comes to our inheritance, you and I must be able to give if we want to receive, and we must be able to receive if we want to give.

Oftentimes, believers have just as much difficulty in receiving as the rich ruler had in giving. Many people are programmed in their thinking that they can give, yet they don't know how to receive. In reality, they're not communicating because there's not a flow of giving and receiving.

Step 3—Don't wait until heaven to withdraw from your account.

When we read in 1 Timothy 6:19, "Laying up in store for themselves a good foundation against the time to come," it's not talking about laying up in heaven so you can use it when you get there.

The same applies to Matthew 6:19-20—

"Lay not up for yourselves treasures upon earth, where moth and rust doth corrupt, and where thieves break through and steal: But lay up for yourselves treasures in heaven, where neither moth nor rust doth corrupt, and where thieves do not break through nor steal."

Here, the word *treasures* means "a protected storehouse." In some places in the Greek, it's used the way we would use the word *coffin*—absolutely sealed forever and buried in the ground.

Why would you and I need to build up a big bank account in heaven and not touch it until we get there, anyway? There's nothing in heaven that costs anything. Everything is already paid for. So we certainly won't need a penny of our inheritance once we step over into the sweet by-and-by.

No, where we need it is right here in the tough here-and-now!

Step 4—Know how much is in your account.

Can you imagine going to the bank to withdraw some money from your checking account one day and not having a clue how much money you have in it?

"Hello, I'd like to take some money out of my account, please."

"Certainly, Mr. Copeland. How much would you like?"

"Oh, I don't know...$100 would be fine... well, maybe $1,000."

"So...do you want $100 or $1,000?"

"Actually, a million would be nice—How much do you figure I could have?"

You and I ought to be keeping records of our heavenly accounts, just as we do with our earthly accounts—not to prove to God that we give, but for our own information. It is our money, remember.

We also need to keep in mind that—just as with most earthly banking accounts—our heavenly accounts gain interest. That is, God multiplies the seed we sow—the things we give.

Jesus taught His disciples about something I call the noncompromised seed. In Mark 10:29-30, He said:

> Truly, I tell you, there is no one who has given up and left house or brothers or sisters or mother or father or children or lands, for My sake and for the Gospel's

who will not receive a hundred times as much now in this time—houses and brothers and sisters and mothers and children and lands, with persecutions—and in the age to come, eternal life *(The Amplified Bible).*

When we sow, God increases us. We never run out. We cannot empty our accounts.

Step 5—Write down the amount you're withdrawing.

Again, in comparing our heavenly account with an earthly one, if we wanted to make a withdrawal from a checking account, we wouldn't walk into the bank lobby and fall down on the floor in front of a teller and start crying…"Oh, please give me my money… please, just give me my money! My family is hungry, my rent is due…can't someone give me my money, please?"

No, we would fill out a withdrawal slip or write a check, hand it to the teller, then wait for him to give us our money.

The point is, once we decide on the amount we want to withdraw, we need to write it down. Then, as we look at that amount or whatever we've written, we need to keep looking at The Word as well.

Don't just meditate on the withdrawal slip—meditate on God's Word, too!

"Lord, I'm going to pay off this car...I'm going to pay off this house—I don't know how it will happen, but Mark 11:23 says I can have what I say, and I say, 'In Jesus' Name, my car is paid...my house is paid....'"

Step 6—Don't let the devil talk you out of it.

Once you've laid hold of the amount you're believing to receive from your heavenly account, and you've laid hold of God's Word on it—stick to it!

Do not let the devil talk you out of what rightfully belongs to you.

THEN...

Step 7—Praise...Praise...Praise!

Every morning when you wake up, say— "Glory to God! I thank You, Lord, for (whatever you're believing for) that's coming out of my heavenly account! It's mine! Harvesting angels of God, in the Name of Jesus, you go get what's mine...you go get it and bring it to me."

And every time the devil says, *You're not going to get that*, you say, "Satan, you thief and you liar, by the authority of the Name of Jesus and by His blood, I have what I'm believing for, and you're not touching it! It's already in the heavenly account my Father set up for me, and according to Matthew 6:19-20, you cannot touch it!"

Then sing, shout, dance—rejoice!—before the Lord.

While we may have been raised to think we are the ones hard-pressed to get anything from God, it is really God who has had a hard time getting us to receive what He has already given to us—sonship and inheritance.

We have obtained redemption. We have obtained an inheritance. It's time we realize our full identity as sons and daughters of Almighty God. It's time we shake off the misconceptions of man and the deceptions of the devil, and receive what is rightfully ours. It is time we take hold of our full inheritance—now!

God's not trying to keep anything good from us. He's doing everything He can to get it to us...and yes, that includes motorcycles.

You know, my parents never did get me that motorcycle I had wanted. But God knew my heart. I never stopped dreaming, either— in spite of all the reasons I was told I couldn't have one.

Several years later, Gloria and I and the children came home from a meeting one day. And as we rounded the last corner and drove up to our house, there was a man sitting on the front porch. In his hand was the title to his motorcycle. He wanted me to have it.

That day, God saw to it that the dream of a 6-year-old boy came to pass.

As a born-again child of the King, *you* have an inheritance. Step out in faith and begin to receive all of it, right now! It's yours!

Prayer for Salvation and Baptism in the Holy Spirit

Heavenly Father, I come to You in the Name of Jesus. Your Word says, "Whosoever shall call on the name of the Lord shall be saved" (Acts 2:21). I am calling on You. I pray and ask Jesus to come into my heart and be Lord over my life according to Romans 10:9-10: "If thou shalt confess with thy mouth the Lord Jesus, and shalt believe in thine heart that God hath raised him from the dead, thou shalt be saved. For with the heart man believeth unto righteousness; and with the mouth confession is made unto salvation." I do that now. I confess that Jesus is Lord, and I believe in my heart that God raised Him from the dead.

I am now reborn! I am a Christian—a child of Almighty God! I am saved! You also said in Your Word, "If ye then, being evil, know how to give good gifts unto your children: HOW MUCH MORE shall your heavenly Father give the Holy Spirit to them that ask him?" (Luke 11:13). I'm also asking You to fill me with the Holy Spirit. Holy Spirit, rise up within me as I praise God. I fully expect to speak with other tongues as You give me the utterance

(Acts 2:4). In Jesus' Name. Amen!

Begin to praise God for filling you with the Holy Spirit. Speak those words and syllables you receive—not in your own language, but the language given to you by the Holy Spirit. You have to use your own voice. God will not force you to speak. Don't be concerned with how it sounds. It is a heavenly language!

Continue with the blessing God has given you and pray in the spirit every day.

You are a born-again, Spirit-filled believer. You'll never be the same!

Find a good church that boldly preaches God's Word and obeys it. Become part of a church family who will love and care for you as you love and care for them.

We need to be connected to each other. It increases our strength in God. It's God's plan for us.

Make it a habit to watch the *Believer's Voice of Victory* television broadcast and become a doer of the Word, who is blessed in his doing (James 1:22-25).

About the Author

Kenneth Copeland is co-founder and president of Kenneth Copeland Ministries in Fort Worth, Texas, and best-selling author of books that include *How to Discipline Your Flesh* and *Honor—Walking in Honesty, Truth and Integrity.*

Since 1967, Kenneth has been a minister of the gospel of Christ and teacher of God's Word. He is also the artist on award-winning albums such as his Grammy-nominated *Only the Redeemed, In His Presence, He Is Jehovah, Just a Closer Walk* and his most recently released *Big Band Gospel* album. He also co-stars as the character Wichita Slim in the children's adventure videos *The Gunslinger, Covenant Rider* and the movie *The Treasure of Eagle Mountain,* and as Daniel Lyon in the *Commander Kellie and the Superkids*TM videos *Armor of Light* and *Judgment: The Trial of Commander Kellie.* Kenneth also co-stars as a Hispanic godfather in the 2009 movie *The Rally.*

With the help of offices and staff in the United States, Canada, England, Australia, South Africa, Ukraine and Singapore, Kenneth is fulfilling his vision to boldly preach the uncompromised WORD of God from the top of this world, to the bottom, and all the way around. His ministry reaches millions of people worldwide through daily and Sunday TV broadcasts, magazines, teaching audios and videos, conventions and campaigns, and the World Wide Web.

Learn more about Kenneth Copeland Ministries
by visiting our website at **kcm.org**

We're Here for You!®

Your growth in God's WORD and victory in Jesus are at the very center of our hearts. In every way God has equipped us, we will help you deal with the issues facing you, so you can be the **victorious overcomer** He has planned for you to be.

The mission of Kenneth Copeland Ministries is about all of us growing and going together. Our prayer is that you will take full advantage of all The LORD has given us to share with you.

Wherever you are in the world, you can watch the *Believer's Voice of Victory* broadcast on television (check your local listings), the Internet at kcm.org or on our digital Roku channel.

Our website, **kcm.org,** gives you access to every resource we've developed for your victory. And, you can find contact information for our international offices in Africa, Asia, Australia, Canada, Europe, Ukraine and our headquarters in the United States.

Each office is staffed with devoted men and women, ready to serve and pray with you. You can contact the worldwide office nearest you for assistance, and you can call us for prayer at our U.S. number, +1-817-852-6000, 24 hours every day!

We encourage you to connect with us often and let us be part of your everyday walk of faith!

Jesus Is LORD!

Kenneth and Gloria Copeland